AMIRE'S UNFORGETTABLE JOURNEY TO THE

GL○BAL BLACK
IMPACT SUMMIT

AMIRE BEN SALMI

I Am
PUBLISHING

AMIRE'S UNFORGETTABLE JOURNEY TO THE

GLOBAL BLACK IMPACT SUMMIT

Published by I AM Publishing

Copyright © 2024 Amire Ben Salmi

Paperback ISBN: 978-1-915862-40-2
Hardback ISBN: 978-1-915862-41-9

DEDICATION

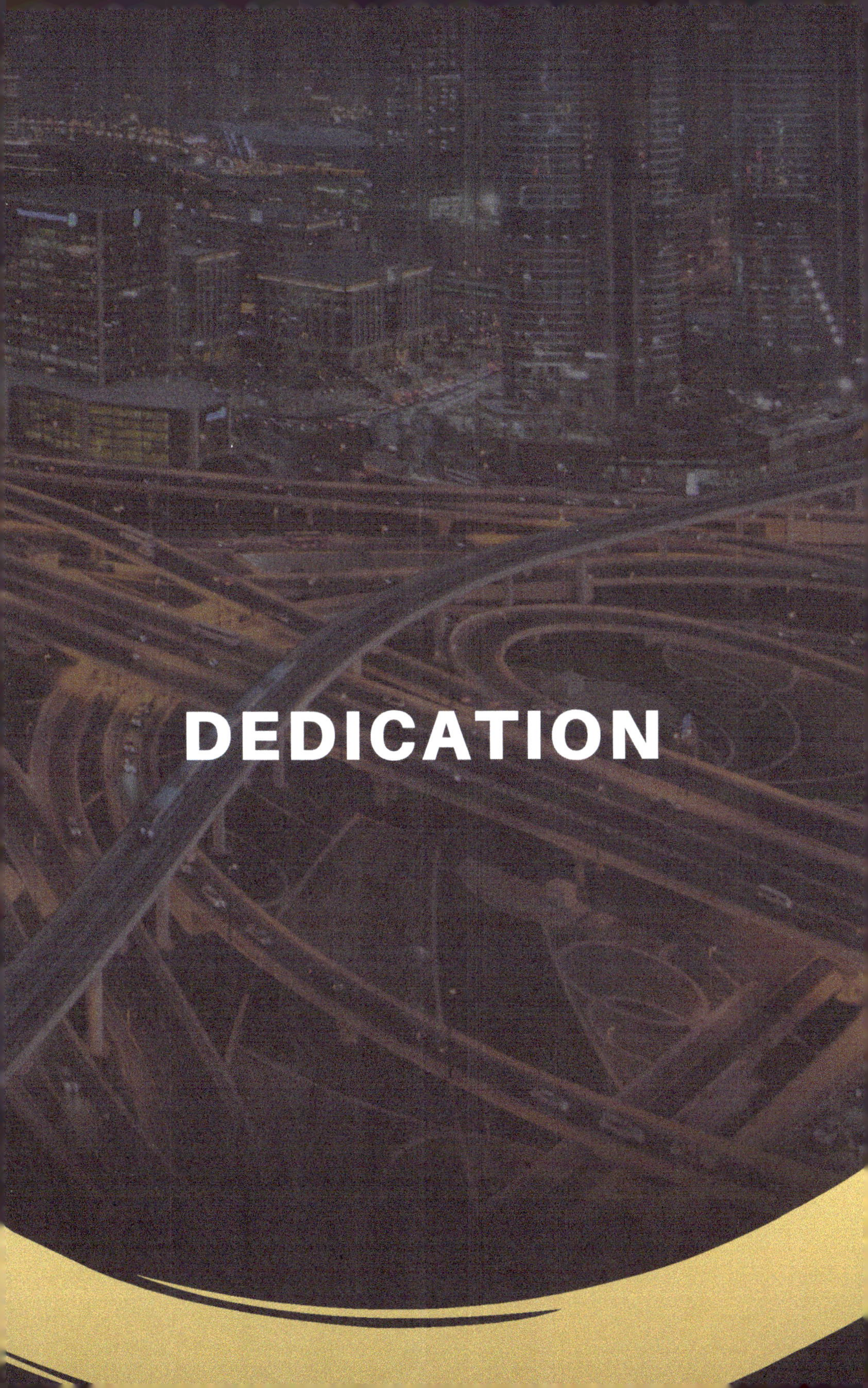

DEDICATION

This book is dedicated to the resilient and inspiring youth of the Global Black Impact Summit 2024 community. To every child who dreams of a brighter future and believes in the power of education, unity, and determination to transform their world. May my story remind you that no matter your age, you have the power to make a difference. Dream big, stay curious, and work together to create a brighter future for everyone.

"

Dreams do come

True

AMIRE'S UNFORGETTABLE JOURNEY TO

THE GLOBAL BLACK
IMPACT SUMMIT

ACKNOWLEDGEMENTS

ACKNOWLEDGEMENT

I extend my heartfelt gratitude to the incredible Asha Lalai, whose huge heart and unwavering support introduced me and my family to the Global Black Impact Summit 2024 and the Black Impact Foundation. Your kindness and dedication to fostering connections have been invaluable.

Special thanks to Ivolaine De Nobrega, another pillar of support, whose generosity and passion have inspired us all. Your contributions to our family are deeply appreciated.

We are immensely grateful to the board members of the Black Impact Foundation for their leadership and vision: Clarence Seedorf, Chairman, NJ Ayuk, Vice-Chair, Vincent Hooplot, the Board Members Ivolaine De Nobrega, Board Member Wilma Gillis-Burleson, Board Member Ashnie Bisalsingh, Board Secretary Miquel Hooplot, Treasurer.

A special thanks to all the incredible speakers who shared their wisdom and experiences at the Global Black Impact Summit 2024:
Clarence Seedorf Chairman of the Black Impact Foundation. NJ Ayuk Vice-Chair of the Black Impact Foundation. Novi Brown Producer, Director, Actor. Hon. Jason Hayward JP MP Minister of Economy and Labour Bermuda Government. Luol Deng President South Sudan Basketball Federation. Amadou Gallo Fall President Basketball Africa League. Olakunle Williams Chief Executive Officer Tetracore Energy Group. Eddie Kadi Comedian and TV Personality. Auriel Rawlings Thought-Leader Regional Inclusion Advisor for the UK Government Foreign Commonwealth & Development Office, Board Member and Mentor. Alycia M. Powell Founder Champions for Impact Arno Peperkoorn, Chief Talent Officer Omnicom Media Group. Bree West Executive Producer, Showrunner, Writer & Director, OCTET Productions and her husband Chuck West, Executive Producer, Showrunner, President and CEO, OCTET Productions. Jefferson Osei Co-founding Director Co-owner & CEO Daily Paper. Pravini Baboeram Co-founder of 7th Gen Creatives, Decolonial Community Organizer Creative Producer.

ACKNOWLEDGEMENT

Dr. Betty Uribe, Former Managing Director JP Morgan Chase Author and United Nations Ambassador for Peace & Human Rights. Allié Merrick McGuire, Co-Founder, AwareNow Media & Editor-in-Chief, AwareNow Magazine. Atong Amos, Founder & CEO, Triple A Services & Petroleum. Dr. Ehsan Natour Internationally Renowned Heart Surgeon, Author and Social Entrepreneur. Sara Rehane Founder of AFRICA FC, World Cup Senior Manager FIFA. Rania Rostom, Head of Global Marketing & Communications, GE. Diana Matroos Presenter, Interviewer & Journalist. Sage Gallon Artist, Painter & Entertainer. Dr. Obari Cartman President, Chicago Association of Black Psychologists. Mary Mugo CEO, Edukans Kenya. David Pappoe Jr President, African Energy Chamber Ghana and Chief Executive Officer, Energas West Africa Limited. My mum Sabrina Ben Salmi FRSA Founder, Dreaming Big Together Publishing, Family Advocate & Publisher, my big sister Lashai Ben Salmi FRSA, TEDx Speaker, Co-Founder of Hallyu Con, Distinguished Korean Wave Representative, Cultural Connectivity Specialist & Content Creator, my big brother Tray-Sean Ben Salmi FRSA, TEDx Speaker, Founder of Influencer Publishing & Financial Education for Teens, my big sister Yasmine Ben Salmi, Founder of The Choice Is Yours Publishing and my big brother Paolo Ben Salmi Founder of The Big Question and myself Amire Ben Salmi aka Mr Intelligent, Founder of I AM Publishing House. Joel Nzali Co-Founding Partner - Board President, Batsela Holding Group. Ruqaya Kalla Entrepreneur, Mentor, and Holistic Well-being Advocate. Thando Magumise Founder & CD. Ntombi Couture Dubai, Co-Founder, Africa Fashionweek Middle East. Isaac Kwaku Fokuo Jr. Head of Middle East and Africa, Propagate Content. Barbro Ciakudia Senior Manager, Business Development and CSR, AMEA Power. Mayowa Adegoke International Journalist and Speaker. Mako Nyakotyo Operations Executive - DMCC Coffee Centre. Joe Osawaye Chief Inspiration Officer Kiza Culture & Vibe. Amena Bakr Senior Research Analyst and Lastly, I would like to share a comment that was shared at the Global Black Impact said about our family

"Our deepest appreciation goes to Sabrina Ben Salmi and her remarkable children, Lashai, Tray-Sean, Yasmine, Paolo and Amire. Your journey and achievements are a testament to the power of family, love, and determination. Thank you for sharing your story and inspiring others to dream big and strive for excellence." quote from the event

AMIRE'S UNFORGETTABLE JOURNEY TO
THE GLOBAL BLACK
IMPACT SUMMIT

INTRODUCTION

INTRODUCTION

Hi there, my name is Amire Ben Salmi, and I am the youngest of the of the Ben Salmi siblings. I am an 11-year-old with a big heart and an even bigger imagination. I have always been curious about the world and for many years one of my dream destinations was to visit Dubai, UAE. Alongside my siblings: Lashai, Tray-Sean, Yasmine, and Paolo, and under the loving guidance of our mum, Sabrina Ben Salmi we embarked on an incredible adventure that changed our lives forever. This is the story of our amazing experience attending the Global Black Impact Summit 2024 - Dubai, UAE an event that celebrates the achievements and contributions of the global Black community. As a family we are blessed to be a blessing to nations, and we thank God for all our blessings daily. The Global Black impact Summit was founded by the legendary former Dutch footballer Clarence Seedorf.

"Let's get into it"

AMIRE'S UNFORGETTABLE JOURNEY TO

THE GLOBAL BLACK IMPACT SUMMIT

CHAPTER 1:
A SPECIAL INVITATION

One sunny morning in our Ben Salmi family household, we were all buzzing with excitement.

.

Mum, had just received an official invitation for Lashai, Mum and Tray-Sean to participate as panellists at the prestigious Global Black Impact Summit 2024, ADDRESS SKYVIEW, DUBAI UNITED ARAB EMIRATES.

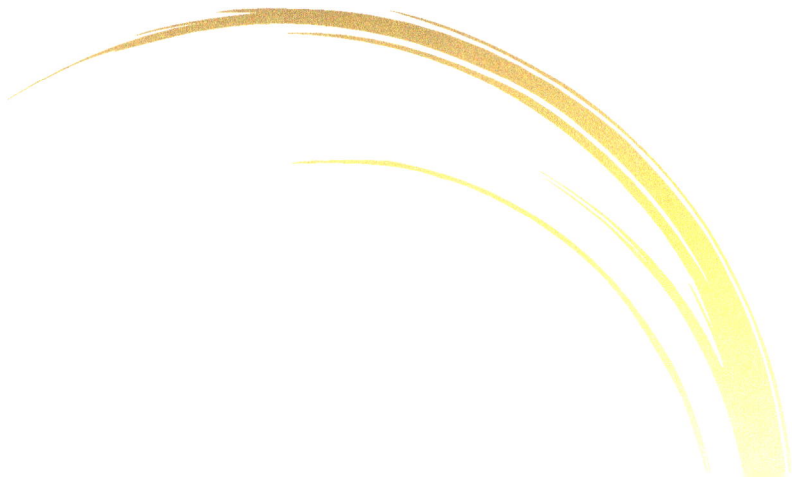

We were excited to thank our incredible family friend Asha Lalai, who kindly introduced our entire family to the amazing Ivolaine De Nobrega and Matshego Njumbuxa from the Global Black Impact Summit team.

.

"The Global Black Impact Summit is an amazing event," and...

"It's a place where leaders, entrepreneurs, and role models from around the world come together to celebrate Black excellence and promote unity." mum explained

My eyes sparkled with anticipation because I had always dreamed of visiting Dubai with my family. Now, we get to mix business (our family mission of servitude leadership) with pleasure.

We are one family, who have 6 dreams and one family mission to touch the hearts and minds of people around the world.

I couldn't wait to see what the summit had in store for us as a family, especially as it was being held in Dubai. Not forgetting the fact that the legendary Dutch former professional footballer and association football manager Clarence Seedorf founded the 'Global Black Impact Summit' and the 'Black Impact Foundation'.

I asked myself, 'How can it get any better than this?..'

Leading up to the Global Black Impact Summit 2024, I found myself counting down the days despite knowing that my family and I were attending. There was a part of me that could not believe that it was going to happen because it sounded too good to be TRUE!...

The night before we flew from London to Dubai I felt both excited and anxious about the flight. I felt so grateful to have the loving support of my family.

The flight was amazing and I even got to meet the pilot, sit in his seat and take an awesome photo. He was so funny and friendly.

It wasn't until we landed in Dubai, that I said to myself 'Wow!... it's really happening'.

When we got out of the airport my jaw dropped! Dubai was hot and all kinds of awesome. Initially mum had told us that we would be staying at an hotel called Easy Hotel, however our taxi ride was much longer than anticipated, so I had a feeling that Mum and Lashai had a surprise in store for us. During our journey we saw so many incredible landmarks such as the Dubai Frame, Dubai Mall, Museum of the Future and the Burj Khalifa etc. We followed signs to a theme park area and they even had Legoland Dubai and then we pulled up to our hotel called 'ROVE on the Park'. It was epic! We had a heated swimming pool, gaming area, gym and so much more. We had two family rooms one for me and my big brothers Tray-Sean and Paolo and the other room was for Mum and my two big sisters Lashai and Yasmine.

AMIRE'S UNFORGETTABLE JOURNEY TO

THE GLOBAL BLACK
IMPACT SUMMIT

CHAPTER 2:
ARRIVING AT THE SUMMIT

The morning of the summit arrived, and two drivers were sent to collect us from our hotel. Me, Tray-Sean and Paolo went into one car while Mum, Lashai and Yasmine got into the other one. We were roughly 30-45 minutes from the venue and the journey was epic. We drove behind each other and we saw amazing landmarks and so many supercars. As we pulled up to the prestigious ADDRESS SKYVIEW Hotel, a film crew filmed our arrival and we were welcomed like Royalty. We found ourselves in a grand venue filled with a host of inspiring people and then greeted by our family friend Asha Lalai.

We quickly realised that we were
a part of something truly special.
We each glanced at each other
and there was a silent
communication that communicated
a thousand words without
uttering a single word.

I quickly noticed the diversity of the attendees. There were leaders from Finance, Health, Oil and Gas, Property Investment, Fashion, Commerce, Education and Sports etc. We were taken to the VIP Speaker room to leave our bags and then introduced to the legendary Clarence Seedorf who was very kind and funny. We were then taken to our table to be seated in the main hall. It was at that moment I realised that I was in a room surrounded by giants, trailblazers, movers and shakers who looked like me and my family. This made me feel special inside because representation matters. We were all united by a common goal:

to foster black excellence, connections and to promote equality within the global Black community.

The Global Black Impact Summit 2024 was officially opened by their chairman the legendary Clarence Seedorf and then Hon. Jason Hayward JP MP Minister of Economy and Labour Bermuda Government delivered a thought provoking speech ahead of the panels and speeches.

AMIRE'S UNFORGETTABLE JOURNEY TO

THE GLOBAL BLACK
IMPACT SUMMIT

CHAPTER 3:
THE VISIONARY AWARD SURPRISE

As the day turned into night we were asked to get changed into evening wear for the Black Impact Foundation Gala, Our family sat at a table with the inspirational David Pappoe Jr and Mako Nyakotyo. Then we were served an elegant three-course meal fit for Royalty. Then they started to announce awards... they called out

"Sabrina Ben Salmi"

It was so funny because our Mum was in shock and she just sat there clapping until she realised it was her they were calling. Mum did not get up straight away, so Tray-Sean and I took Mum by the hand to lead her to the stage.

We watched proudly as
our Mum received a
surprise Visionary Award
for her incredible
contributions to society.

.

Mum's eyes welled with tears of joy as she accepted the award presented to her by our eldest daughter Lashai Ben Salmi.

.

Only four awards were
given that night, which
added to the shock!...

CONGRATULATIONS TO THE BLACK
IMPACT FOUNDATION WINNERS

- Trailblazer. Award - NJ Ayuk
- Visionary Award - Sabrina Ben Salmi
- Legacy Award - Luol Deng
- Impact Award - Amadou Gallo Fall

"This award isn't just for me," Mum said, looking at her children. "It's for all of us. It's a reminder that we can all make a difference."

CHAPTER 4:
ON STAGE WITH LEGENDS

During the summit, there was so much to learn from all the speeches, panels and interviews. Lashai was the moderator for a panel that Tray-Sean also participated in as a panellist, Then Mum took to the stage as a panellist in a separate panel. During the break, I was with my brother Paolo and we had an awesome conversation with the legendary Clarence Seedorf and David Pappoe Jr. As a result of that conversation the legendary Clarence Seedorf told us to share our conversation from the stage when the summit resumes!... but wait - we were not initially apart of the summit. I said to myself this cannot be happening.

When the summit resumed the next panel speakers were welcomed to the stage...

but then the legendary Clarence Seedorf lifted his hand and stopped the scheduled panel. I looked at him and froze and then he called me, Lashai, Tray-Sean, Yasmine and Paolo to the stage to have an impromptu fireside chat along with the incredible Lady Mayowa Adegoke. My tummy did a 360 turn. I grabbed my books 'I AM A Leader and Amire The Billionaire' and smiled.

It was at that moment that I knew that our lives would never be the same again. I said to myself:

'We are blessed to be a blessing to nations'.

Paolo and I shared elements of our conversation with the legendary Clarence Seedorf and David Pappoe Jr, and then each of my each of my siblings were asked to speak.

We will cherish that memory for a lifetime.

CHAPTER 5:
LESSONS LEARNED

Throughout the summit, Mum, my siblings and I listened to all the wisdom shared by various speakers and panels.

.

We learned about the critical issues facing their community and discovered ways to create positive change.

We listened to stories of success and perseverance, and we met inspiring role models who encouraged us to pursue their dreams.

Some conversations led to us finding mentors, friends, a clothing brand collaboration and even a new book series based on the attendees at the summit. The opportunities were endless.

My family and I realised that the Global Black Impact Summit was more than an ordinary event, it was a mission to amplify Black excellence and advocate for equity. It was a community where we could all grow and thrive as a family. As a family, we had never been a part of a community until that moment.

We felt empowered and motivated to contribute to this mission in our own way.

CHAPTER 6:
SHARE, CONNECT, GROW

As the summit came to an end, I reflected on the incredible experiences I had shared with my family.

I felt a deep sense of pride and empowerment because for the very first time in my entire life my family and I were in a room filled with black excellence from around the world,

Across every sector and it was at that moment I knew that I was unstoppable. I was surrounded by giants and I could now see so much further because I now stand on their shoulders. I then said to myself:

'Thank you God for blessing me and my family, we are ready to serve nations'.

The summit taught me the importance of sharing knowledge, connecting with others, and growing together as a community. My family and I knew that we would grow from this day forth and we also felt inspired to pour into the community too.

I made a promise to myself to always strive for excellence and to help others along the way.

I knew that, with unity and determination, the Global Black Impact community could overcome any challenge and achieve great things.

Representation matters!

I now know that I can be, do and have whatever I desire.

Because we become what we see is possible and...

I saw life with a totally different perspective after attending the Global Black Impact Summit 2024 and my life will never be the same again.

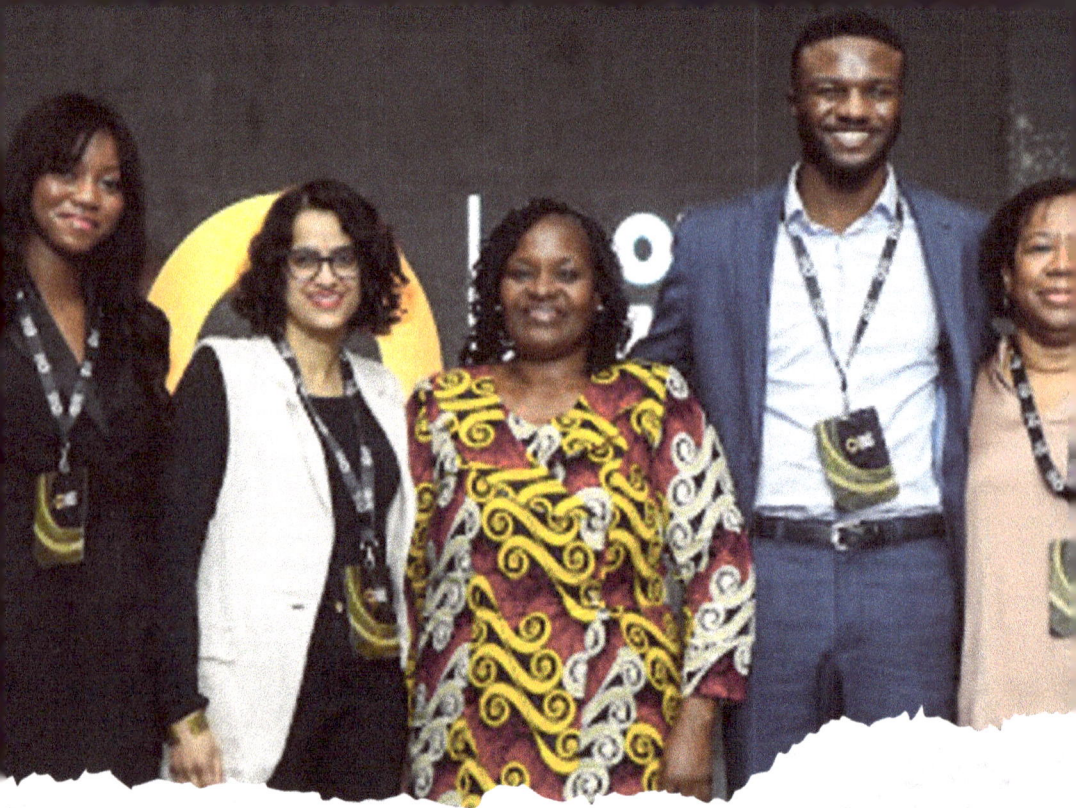

AMIRE'S UNFORGETTABLE JOURNEY TO

THE GLOBAL BLACK
IMPACT SUMMIT

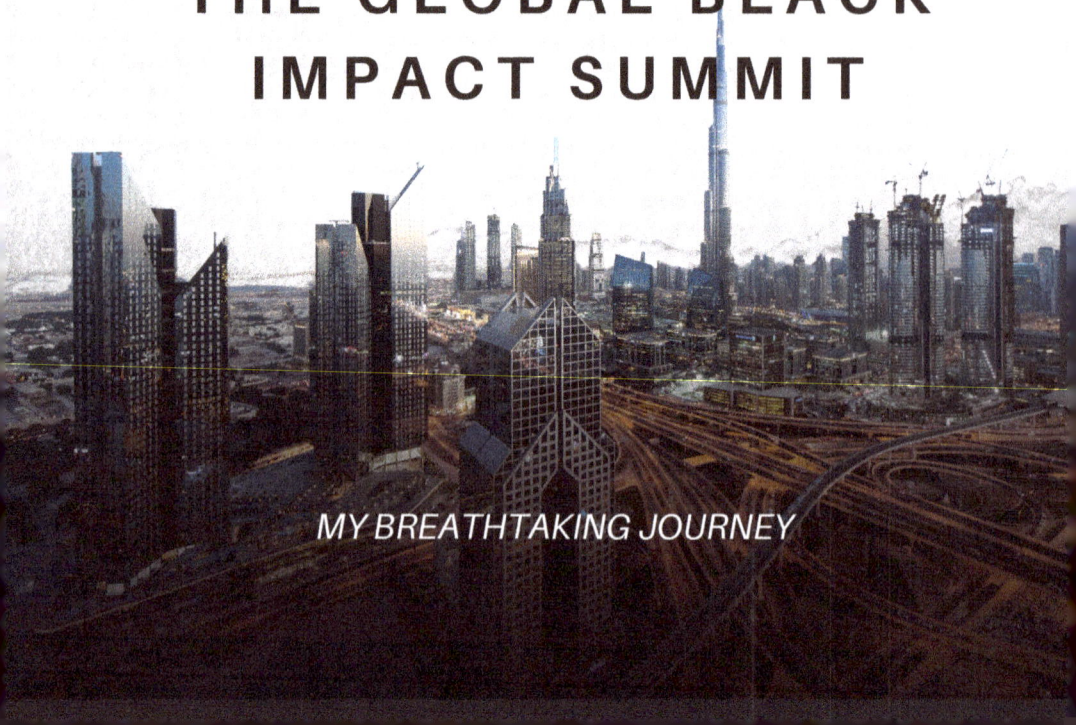

MY BREATHTAKING JOURNEY

EPILOGUE:
A MEMORY TO CHERISH

Returning home, my family and I carried with us the memories of the Global Black Impact Summit 2024.

The event left an indelible mark on our hearts, inspiring us to make a bigger difference everywhere we go.

We could each feel the warmth of this community and we were blessed to form long-lasting relationships and friendships that felt like family as a result of attending.

I often think back to the moment I stood on stage with my four siblings and the legendary Clarence Seedorf and Mrs. Mayowa Adegoke. It is a memory that I will cherish for a lifetime, it is a reminder that I, too, can be a changemaker and a beacon of hope for others even at the young age of eleven.

Key Learnings from the Global Black Impact Summit 2024

1. The Power of Unity:
The summit emphasised the importance of unity within the global Black community. By coming together, sharing experiences, and supporting one another, we can create a stronger, more resilient community capable of overcoming any challenge.

2. The Importance of Ethical Governance:

Speakers like NJ Ayuk highlighted the need for ethical governance and transparent practices, particularly in the energy and mining sectors. Ensuring that resources are managed responsibly and equitably can lead to sustainable development and improved quality of life for all.

3. Advocacy for Education:
The summit underscored
the critical role of
education in empowering
the next generation. By
prioritising educational
opportunities over
outdated practices such as
child labour, we can equip
young people with the tools
they need to drive positive
change and innovation.

4. Addressing Corruption: Corruption remains a significant barrier to progress in many African countries. Discussions at the summit focused on the detrimental effects of corruption and the urgent need for reforms to ensure resources reach those who need them most.

5. Embracing Diversity in Leadership:

The event showcased the diverse leadership within the Black community, spanning various sectors such as health, commerce, education, sports, and more. This diversity is a strength that can drive innovative solutions and inclusive growth.

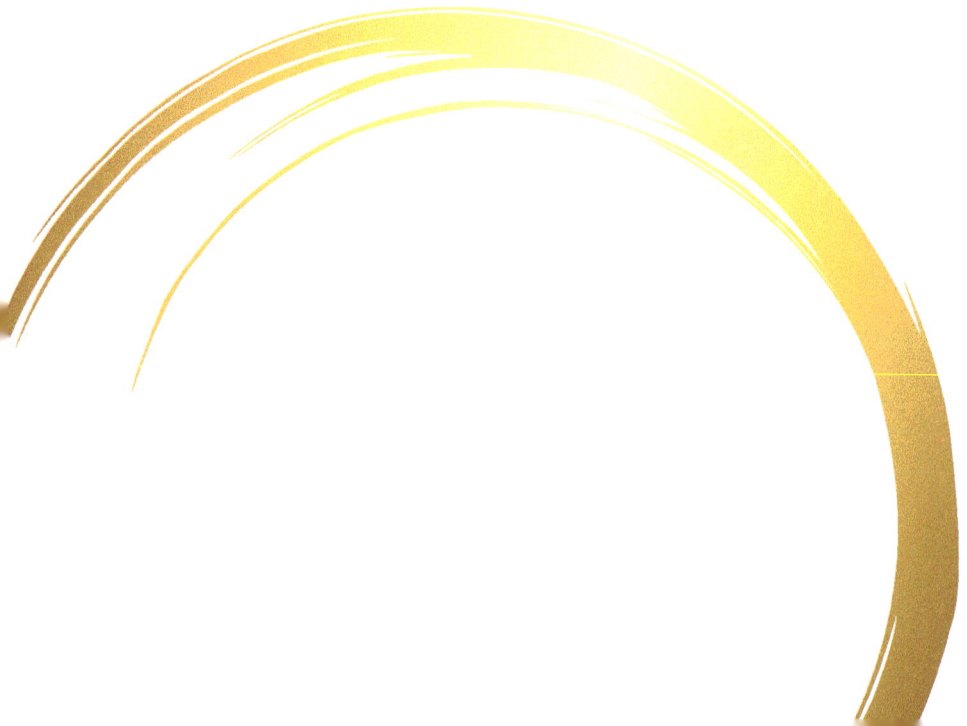

6. The Role of Role Models: Having visible, successful role models from the Black community is crucial. Leaders and speakers at the summit, such as the legendary Clarence Seedorf, David Pappoe Jr and Luol Deng, serve and many more as powerful inspirations, demonstrating that excellence and success are achievable.

7. Creating Opportunities for Growth:

The summit highlighted the importance of creating and seizing opportunities for growth within the Black community. By fostering connections and partnerships, individuals and organisations can drive meaningful initiatives that benefit all.

8. Networking and Collaboration: The event provided a platform for networking and collaboration, encouraging attendees to form partnerships that can lead to impactful projects and initiatives. Building a strong network of like-minded individuals and organisations is key to driving collective progress.

9. Promoting Equality:
A central theme of the summit was the ongoing fight for equality. Speakers and attendees discussed strategies for advocating for equity and ensuring that everyone, regardless of their background, has access to opportunities and resources.

10. Inspiring Empowerment: Finally, the summit served as a powerful source of inspiration and empowerment. By celebrating achievements and sharing stories of resilience and success, the event inspired attendees to believe in their potential and take action to make a difference in their communities and beyond.

AMIRE'S UNFORGETTABLE JOURNEY TO
THE GLOBAL BLACK
IMPACT SUMMIT

CONCLUSION

The Global Black Impact Summit 2024 was an enlightening and empowering experience for me and my family. The following day my family and I were guests on a podcast called Mentl hosted by Scott Armstrong and we discussed mums surprise award too.

.

The key learnings from the event will guide us as we continue to strive for excellence, unity, and positive change within our community and beyond.

Our Dubai dream holiday did not end there because mum and Lashai had a trick up their sleeve, they told us that they only stayed at the 'Rove on the Park' Hotel for the event and that we all had to pack so we could checkout. When our taxi arrived we were told that we would be heading to Easy Hotel. The drive was long and the hotel were were staying at was close to the airport. as our taxi drove across a luxuriousbridge leading to a private island for two hotels...

It was at that moment I shouted out I know this hotel, you lied to us - we are not going to Easy Hotel (not that there is anything wrong with Easy Hotel) I saw Mum and Lashai watching YouTube videos about this hotel and it's called RIU. Wow! Our family trip to Dubai just kept getting better and better. Lashai surprised us with a collaboration stay at RIU for the remainder of our stay in Dubai. RIU is an all-inclusive hotel (check out our social media to see our videos).

IIt was all you could eat around the clock, with several restaurants serving breakfast, lunch and dinner and food available throughout the day too. Unlimited. Ice-creams and drinks included three outdoor pools, water sports, a pool table, a disco and water slides what could we ask for? The other highlight of our trip was getting to spend Mum's birthday out exploring the Burj Kalifa, The Frame, Museum of the Future, Souk, the metro, Dubai Mall and so much more. Before returning home we flew to Doha, Qatar and visited an incredible seven-star hotel called Raffles, Doha and got an exclusive tour (check my socials to watch the video).

For more information about the Global Black Impact Summit and the Black Impact Foundation please visit:
www.globalblackimpact.com
&
www.blackimpactfoundation.com

AMIRE

BEN SALMI

GLOBAL BLACK IMPACT SUMMIT 2024

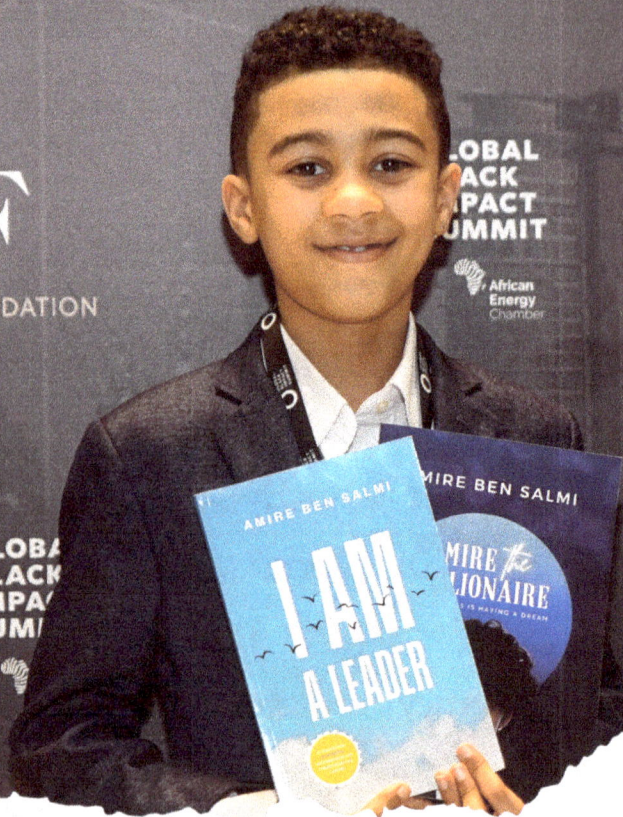

AMIRE'S UNFORGETTABLE JOURNEY TO

THE GLOBAL BLACK
IMPACT SUMMIT

Dubai United Arab Emirates

AFFIRMATIONS

Affirmations are important because they harness the power of positive thinking and self-talk to shape our mindset, improve mental well-being, and influence behavior. Here are some key reasons why affirmations are effective:

1. Rewiring the Brain

Affirmations can reprogram the brain by replacing negative, self-limiting beliefs with empowering ones. When repeated regularly, they create new neural pathways, promoting a more positive and optimistic outlook. This is known as neuroplasticity, the brain's ability to adapt and change in response to new experiences and thoughts.

2. Boosting Confidence and Self-Esteem

By consistently affirming positive statements about ourselves, we build confidence and enhance self-esteem. Positive affirmations encourage self-acceptance, self-love, and a sense of worth, which can help overcome self-doubt and fear of failure.

3. Enhancing Motivation and Focus

Affirmations act as a mental reminder of goals, helping to maintain focus and motivation. Repeating statements like "I am capable of achieving my goals" keeps you aligned with your purpose and reinforces the belief that success is possible.

4. Reducing Stress and Anxiety

Affirmations can shift attention away from negative thoughts, reducing stress and anxiety. Positive self-talk can help calm the mind, combat fear-based thinking, and promote emotional resilience.

5. Promoting a Growth Mindset
Regular use of affirmations
fosters a growth mindset, the
belief that abilities and intelligence
can be developed over time.
Affirmations like "I embrace
challenges and learn from them"
encourage perseverance,
adaptability, and a focus on
improvement rather than
perfection.

6. Improving Overall Well-Being

Affirmations help cultivate a sense of gratitude and positivity, which can enhance emotional well-being. By fostering a habit of speaking kindly to ourselves, affirmations promote happiness, reduce feelings of inadequacy, and create a more positive inner environment.

7. Influencing Behavior

What we believe about ourselves often dictates how we act. Positive affirmations, by changing how we think, can inspire us to take actions aligned with those beliefs. This can lead to better habits, improved relationships, and greater personal growth.

In summary, affirmations help shift our mindset, build self-confidence, improve mental health, and drive positive actions, ultimately helping us lead more fulfilling and empowered lives.

Say the following affirmations several times a day for the best effect.

I AM BRAVE ENOUGH TO EXPLORE NEW OPPORTUNITIES AND EMBRACE MY JOURNEY WITH CONFIDENCE.

MY IMAGINATION
KNOWS NO
LIMITS, AND I AM
CAPABLE OF
CREATING A
POSITIVE IMPACT
ON THE WORLD.

I CELEBRATE THE RICHNESS OF MY HERITAGE AND THE GLOBAL CONTRIBUTIONS OF MY COMMUNITY.

WITH THE LOVE
AND SUPPORT OF
MY FAMILY, I CAN
ACHIEVE
ANYTHING I SET
MY MIND TO.

I AM PROUD OF
WHO I AM AND
HONOR THE
GREATNESS
WITHIN ME.

MY CURIOSITY OPENS DOORS TO NEW KNOWLEDGE, EXPERIENCES, AND POSSIBILITIES.

I AM A PART OF A GLOBAL COMMUNITY THAT UPLIFTS, INSPIRES, AND EMPOWERS EACH OTHER.

THROUGH UNITY
AND
COLLABORATION,
WE CAN
OVERCOME ANY
CHALLENGE AND
CREATE LASTING
CHANGE.

I AM AN ESSENTIAL PIECE OF THE LARGER STORY, AND MY VOICE MATTERS.

I AM INSPIRED BY THE ACHIEVEMENTS OF THOSE WHO CAME BEFORE ME AND MOTIVATED TO PAVE MY OWN PATH.

MY DREAMS ARE
VALID, AND I
HAVE THE POWER
TO MAKE THEM A
REALITY.

I EMBRACE EVERY ADVENTURE AS A CHANCE TO GROW, LEARN, AND EVOLVE.

I AM
SURROUNDED BY
LOVE, WISDOM,
AND
ENCOURAGEMEN
T FROM THOSE
WHO BELIEVE IN
ME.

I HONOR MY
ROOTS AND LET
THEM GUIDE ME
TOWARD AN
EXTRAORDINARY
FUTURE.

I AM RESILIENT,
AND EVERY
CHALLENGE I
FACE MAKES ME
STRONGER.

THE
CONTRIBUTIONS
OF MY
COMMUNITY ARE
VALUABLE, AND I
TAKE PRIDE IN
OUR GLOBAL
IMPACT.

I TRUST MY
ABILITY TO
NAVIGATE NEW
EXPERIENCES
WITH GRACE
AND COURAGE.

I AM A BEACON OF LIGHT, SPREADING HOPE AND POSITIVITY WHEREVER I GO.

MY POTENTIAL IS
LIMITLESS, AND I
AM COMMITTED
TO LEAVING A
LASTING
LEGACY.

I AM ON A
JOURNEY OF
GROWTH, AND I
EMBRACE EVERY
MOMENT WITH
AN OPEN HEART.

AMIRE'S UNFORGETTABLE JOURNEY TO

THE GLOBAL BLACK IMPACT SUMMIT

AMIRE'S UNFORGETTABLE JOURNEY TO
THE GLOBAL BLACK IMPACT SUMMIT

MEMORIES

globalblackimpactsumm

CONGRATULATIONS TO
THE WINNERS

Trailblazer Award - NJ Ayuk

Visionary Award - Sabrina Ben Salmi

Legacy Award - Luol Deng

Impact Award - Amadou Gallo Fall

GLOBAL BLACK IMPACT SUMMIT

BLACK LEADERS HONORED AT GBIS 2024

GLOBAL BLACK IMPACT SUMMIT | 27 February 2024 | Address Sky View Dubai, UAE

BIF
BLACK IMPACT FOUNDATION

🖤 Liked by **authoryasminebensalmi** and **10 others**

globalblackimpactsummit The Black Impact Foundation announced the recipients of four prestigious awards presented at the Global Black Impact Summit Gala... more

21 hours ago

globalblackimpactsummit
Dubai, United Arab Emirates

It includes everyone.

CLARENCE SEEDORF
CHAIRMAN OF THE BLACK IMPACT FOUNDATION

8

GLOBAL BLACK IMPACT SUMMIT

NURTURING FUTURE LEADERS:
EMPOWERING BLACK YOUTH FOR EXCELLENCE

27 FEBRUARY 2024 | 15H00 GST

MARY MUGO
Chief Executive Officer
Edukans Kenya

SABRINA BEN SALMI
Family Advocate,
Publisher& Founder
**Dreaming Big
Together Publishing**

LASHAI BEN SALMI
Cultural Connectivity
Specialist, Content Creator,
Korean Wave Representative
& Co-Founder
Hallyu Con

**TRAY-SEAN
BEN SALMI**
TEDx Speaker &
Founder
**Influencer Publishing
& Financial Education
for Teens**

Address Sky View
Dubai, UAE
globalblackimpact.com

REGISTER NOW »

authortrayseanbensalmi I am pleased to share that we
have received an invitation to participate in the Global B...

The Untapped Potential to Unite Our Global Community

DOWNLOAD THE POST EVENT REPORT →

The Untapped Potential to Unite Our Global Community

DOWNLOAD THE POST EVENT REPORT →

The Untapped Potential to Unite Our Global Community

DOWNLOAD THE POST EVENT REPORT →

The Untapped Potential to Unite Our Global Community

DOWNLOAD THE POST EVENT REPORT →

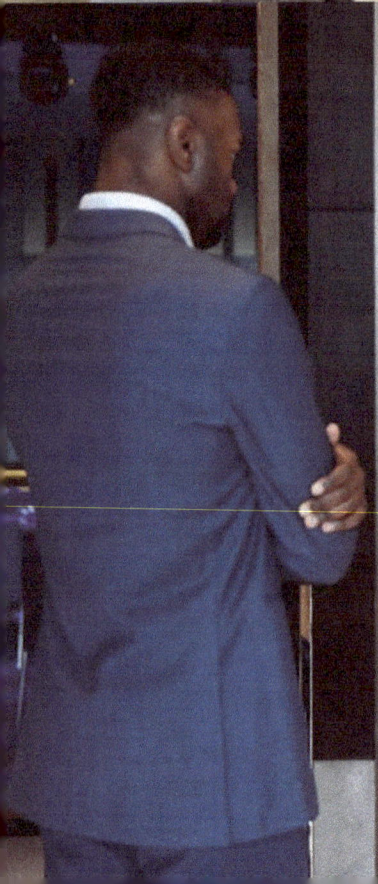

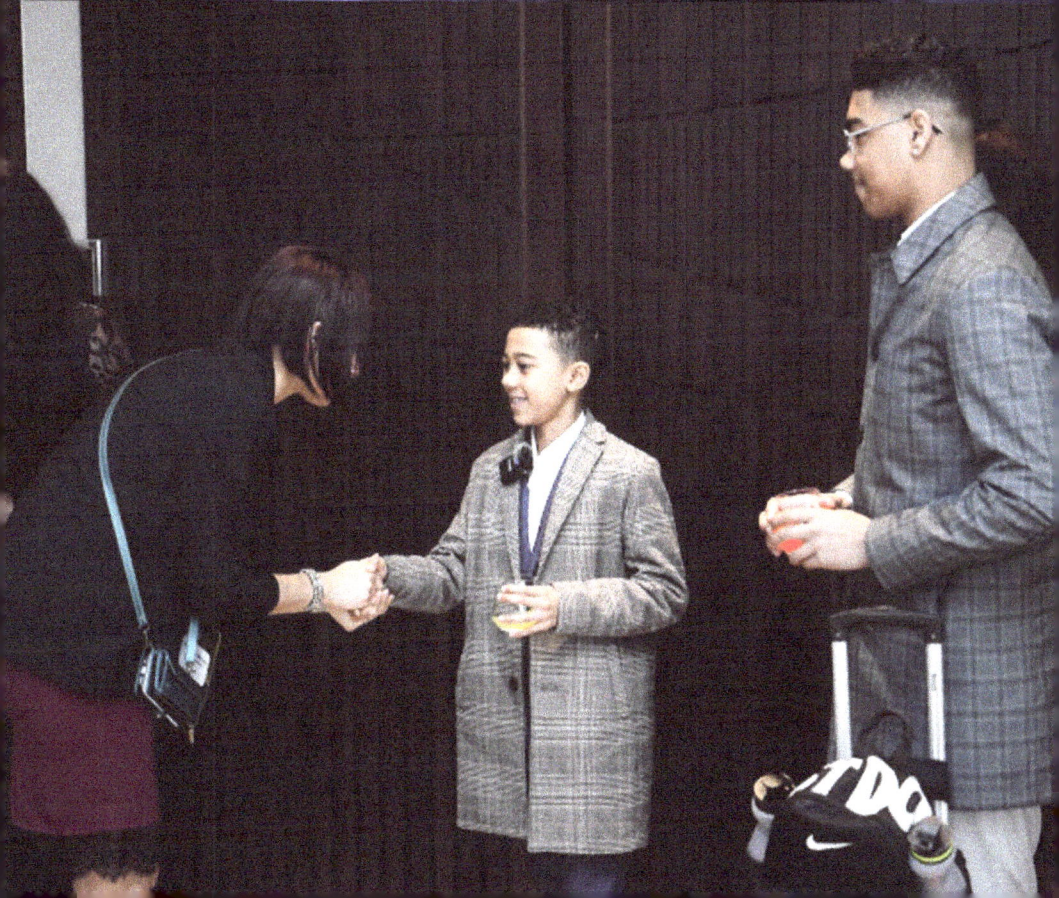

BIF

BLACK IMPACT FOUNDATION

GLOBAL BLACK
IMPACT SUMMIT 2024
VISIONARY AWARD
SABRINA BEN SALMI

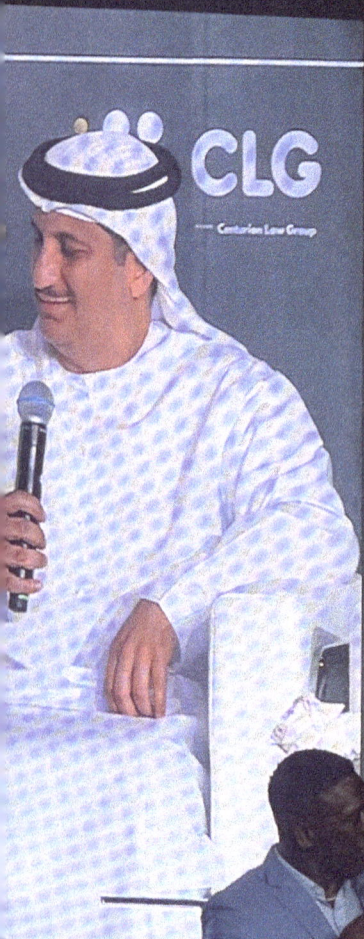

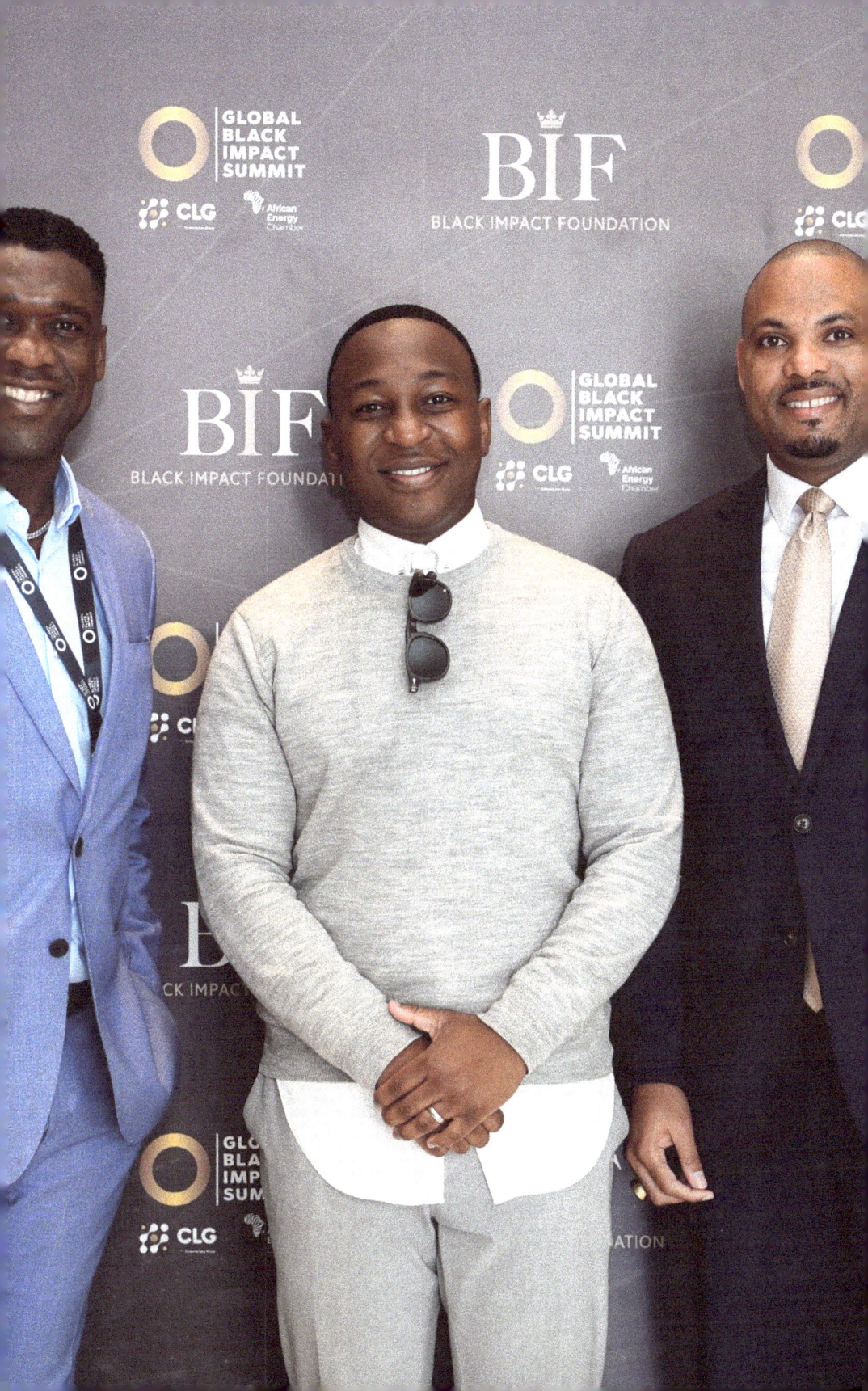

27 February 2024
Dubai United Arab Emirates

#ROVE AROUND THE CITY

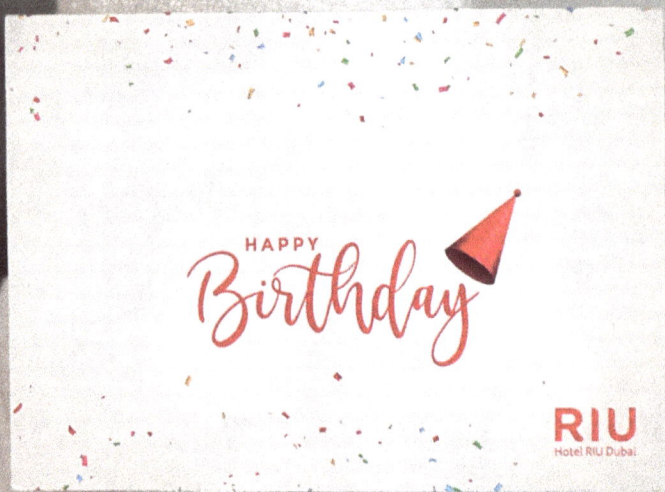

HAPPY
Birthday

RIU
Hotel RIU Dubai

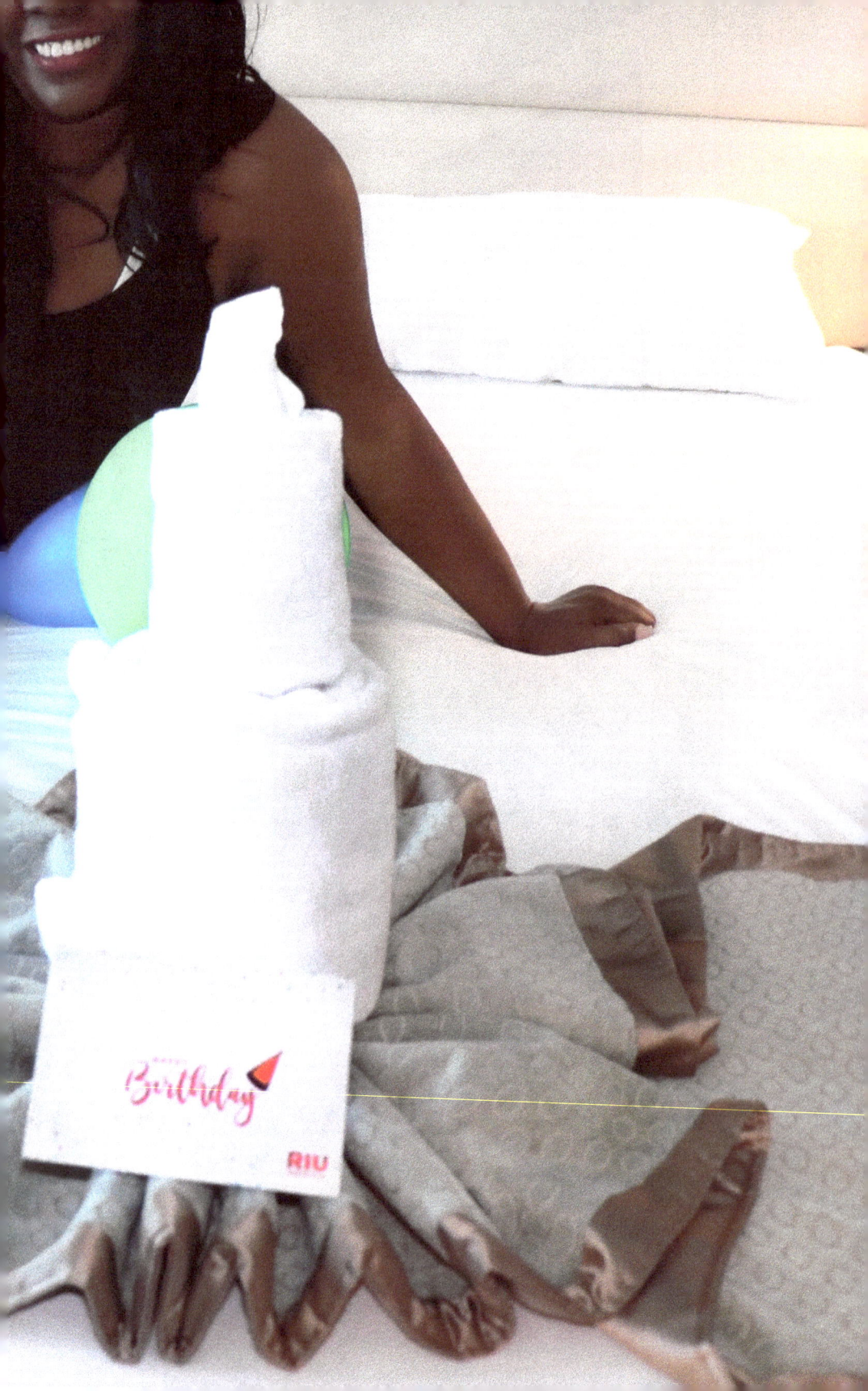

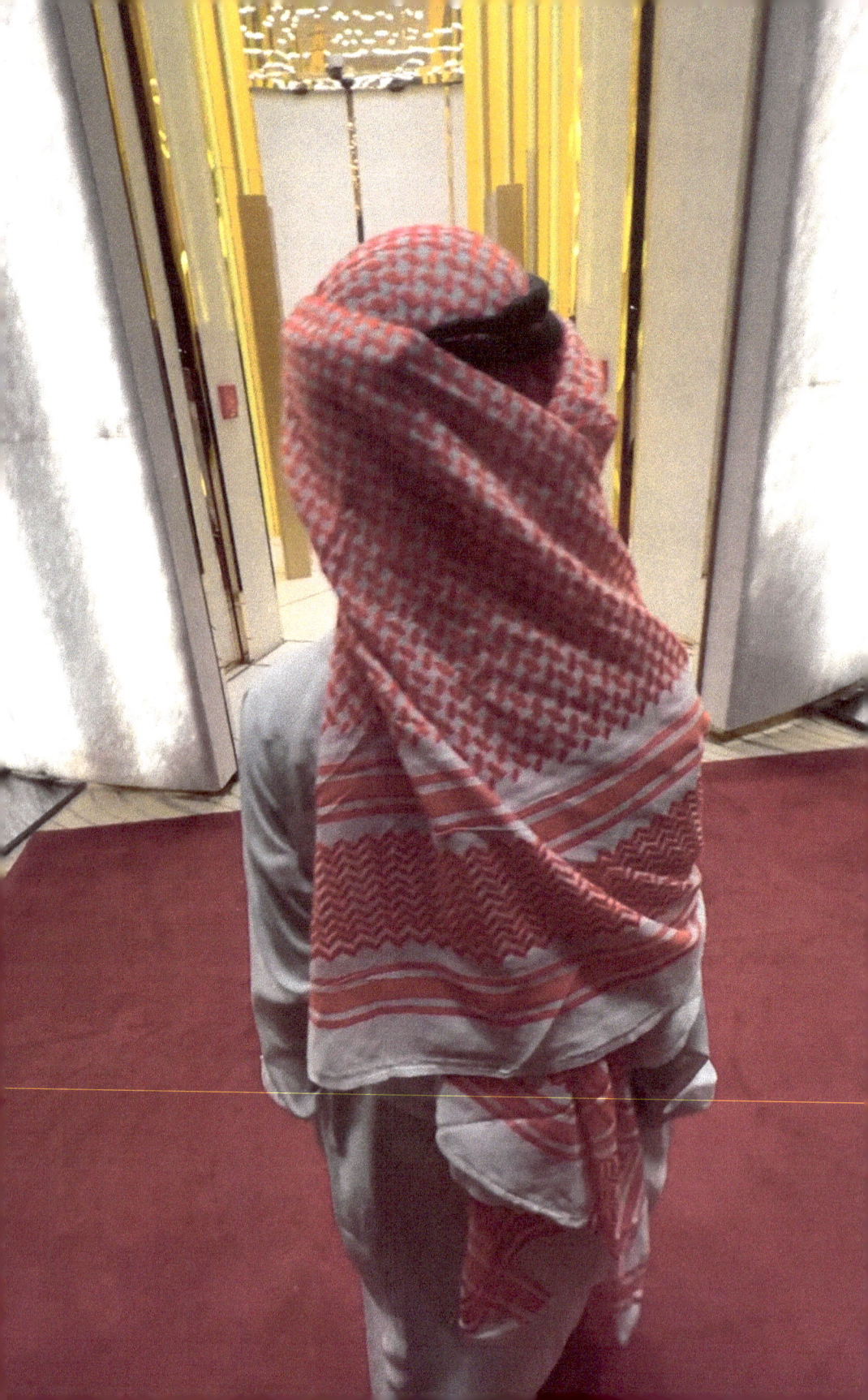

WORDS OF HIS HIGHNESS SHEIKH MOHAMMED
BIN RASHID AL MAKTOUM AS INSCRIBED ON
THE MUSEUM OF THE FUTURE

"The secret to the renewal of life, the evolution of
civilizations, and the development of
humanity is simple: innovation."

"The future belongs to those who can imagine it,
design it, and execute it. It isn't something you
await, but rather create."

"We may not live for hundreds of years, but the
products of our creativity leave a legacy
long after we're gone."

NOTES

NOTES

DREAMS DO COME TRUE

NOTES

NOTES

NOTES

NOTES

DREAMS DO COME TRUE

ABOUT THE AUTHOR

Purpose: To put a smile on the faces of 1 Mission peoples faces starting with you through the teaching of affirmation

Guest speaker at the Global Black Impact Summit founded by the legendary Clarence Seedorf Chairman, Black Impact Foundation: https://globalblackimpact.com/speakers-2023/

Amire was the youngest to become an author in the Ben Salmi family when he published his first book at 3 and a half years old.

I am proud to contribute alongside my four siblings at the UN SOTF Youth Consultations:
https://www.google.co.uk/imgres?imgurl=https%3A%2F%2Fpbs.twimg.com%2Fmedia%2FGBkDkDxXcAA1vxf.jpg&tbnid=V4HhRVYHclmTmM&vet=1&imgrefurl=https%3A%2F%2Ftwitter.com%2Fswissyouthreps%2Fstatus%2F1736423620258218476&docid=eoREzuekyA8Q4M&w=1080&h=1080&hl=en-gb&source=sh%2Fx%2Fim%2Fm4%2F3

Guest speaker alongside his big brother Paolo for an international gathering organised by The Optimisation Hub:
https://www.linkedin.com/posts/the-optimisation-hub_nigeria-nigeria-educatedladership-activity-7124013621767995392-gGKT?utm_source=share&utm_medium=member_ios

Amire Ben Salmi also known as Mr. Intelligent is an 11-year-old award-winning author of a book series called: Because I AM Intelligent: Because I AM Intelligent - 365 Affirmations to Brighten Up Your Day, Because I AM Intelligent – Easy As P.I.E Affirmations and Because I AM Intelligent – I Become What I Affirm. 11-year-old Amire is the founder of I AM Publishing House. Amire is the youngest of the Ben Salmi siblings who are as follows: 24-year-old Lashai Ben Salmi, 19-year-old Tray-Sean Ben Salmi, 17-year-old Yasmine Ben Salmi and 15-year-old Paolo Ben Salmi.

BEN SALMI FAMILY MANTRA
"BEN SALMI TEAMWORK MAKES THE DREAMWORK
We believe that there is no such thing as failure, only feedback.
We also believe that the journey of one thousand miles begins with a single step in the right direction

FAMILY ANTHEM
If you want to be somebody,
If you want to go somewhere,
You better wake up and PAY ATTENTION
I'm ready to be somebody,
I'm ready to go somewhere,
I'm ready to wake up and PAY ATTENTION!
The question is ARE YOU?

Let's STAY CONNECTED

HTTPS://LINKTR.EE/AMIREBENSALMI

in   Amire Ben Salmi

⊙   @AmireGlobalBlackImpact

✉   info@dreamingbigtogether.com

"DREAMS DO COME TRUE"

BLACK
IMPACT
FOUNDATION

Making impact together

Vision
Create a cohesive global black community where black people across the globe are empowered to take control and improve the quality of their lives, assert their value, and be protected from exploitation while building their capacity for social economic independence and social responsibility. Embracing everyone who identifies him/herself as black and everyone with an affinity with the black global community.

Mission
The organisation aims to be a solid pillar and catalyst to empower, build, protect, sustain and further develop an inclusive and equal society through entrepreneurship, education, research and legal support to improve the overall development of, character, sense of worth, and a flourishing value system while encouraging social mobility.

For more information about the Black Impact Foundation please visit their website: www.blackimpactfoundation.com

GLOBAL BLACK IMPACT SUMMIT

A Focus on Black Excellence

The 2024 iteration of the Global Black Impact Summit (GBIS) was a landmark event, centered around the theme "Black Excellence: Unleashing the Unexplored Potential for Global Unity." This theme underscored the Black Impact Foundation's unwavering dedication to the promotion of diversity, equity, and empowerment. It served as a driving force behind this significant gathering, uniting participants with a common mission to fortify and cultivate the worldwide Black community.

Who attends?:

Global leaders, Celebrities, International organizations, NGOs & NPOs, Chief diversity officers, Human resources, Global brands, Entrepreneurs/startups, Investors/banks, Government officials, Students, Educators, Young talented people or leaders, Professionals of any specialties of relevance and so many more.

For more information about the Global Black Impact Summit please visit their website: www.globalblackimpact.com

AFRICAN
ENERGY
CHAMBER

At The Forefront Of The African Energy Industry
We uphold a results-focused business environment for companies operating in Africa's dynamic energy industry. The African Energy Chamber works with indigenous companies throughout the continent in optimizing their reach and networks.

Our partnerships with international dignitaries, executives, and companies allow for relevant servicing to other international entities looking to operate within the continent. The African Energy Chamber brings willing governments and credible businesses together to continuing growth of the African energy sector under international standard business practices.

Africa Is A Powerhouse
With a standard aggregate growth projection expected to continue for the next 15 years, Africa is in the preliminary position of capitalizing on this growth through strategic partnerships and trade. Reduction in barriers of entry in the energy sectors has ushered in more opportunities for new players to profit from our resource rich continent. In developing the energy sector through initiatives, African nations should focus on developing a natural gas market that will service as the foundation of Africa's energy industry. We focus on establishing a strong domestic trading market in this regard.

For more information about the African Energy Chamber please visit their website: www.energychamber.org

**African
Energy
Chamber**

To My Beautiful
Mom

You gave me the confidence that I needed to spread my wings to become the person that I am. You are the only one who stays with me during my ups and downs! You have been such an amazing influence on me since I was born. Thank you for all your life lessons, your love, and your caring ways.

I love you!